This book is dedicated to my grandson
Benny and to **Yotam Ottolenghi**

What do I want to be?

A chef

A series of rhyming books for
young children about different
jobs they might like to do one day

**A rhyming book for young children
by Robert Burkeman**

I love eating good food, maybe you do as well

The best part is the taste and sometimes the smell

I drank my first food, it was milk from my mummy

Some bottled milk also felt good in my tummy

As I got older there was so much to eat

Vegetables and fruit as well as fish and some meat

Soon I ate some desserts then I tried bread and cheese

Dad gave me a knife,
fork and spoon,
he said "Use these"

One day for a treat we went to a restaurant

Mum read me the menu and said
"What do you want?"

I chose pasta
and ice cream,
chocolate of course

Covered with sprinkles and lots of strawberry sauce

Then daddy said a chef prepared all that I ate

It was then
I thought being a chef would be great

Chefs have to learn how to cook all sorts of food

Maybe roasted or grilled, even fried, poached or stewed

I went to chefs school where I became a great cook

One day I even wrote my own recipe book

Greek, Indian, Chinese, sometimes tasty meat pies

French, Spanish, Italian, or burger and fries

I've cooked lots of new dishes all served with a smile

And I still eat in restaurants once in a while

I'm happy and glad about the job that I do

Cook with Love

Being a chef might be the job just for you!

Previously published

What do I want to be?

A teacher
Published on Amazon 17 December 2022

A doctor
Published on Amazon 26 January 2023

A firefighter
Published on Amazon 26 February 2023

A builder
Published on Amazon 28 May 2023

A farmer
Published on Amazon 26 November 2023
Second edition

Watch out!

Coming soon in the series

What do I want to be?

A midwife

A vet

Acknowledgements

Canva Pro

Amazon Kindle Desktop Publishing

Printed in Great Britain
by Amazon